METAPHORS

AN EMOTIONAL JOURNEY

GABRIELA CASINEANU

Copyright © 2020 by Gabriela Casineanu

All rights reserved.

No portion of this book may be reproduced, distributed, or transmitted in any form or by any means, including photocopying or other electronic or mechanical methods, without the prior written permission of the author or publisher, except in the case of brief quotations embodied in reviews and certain other non-commercial uses permitted by copyright law.

Adherence to all applicable laws and regulations is the sole responsibility of the reader and consumer. Neither the author nor the publisher assumes any responsibility or liability whatsoever on behalf of the consumer or reader of this material.

Photos, concept, cover design: Gabriela Casineanu

Editing: Christina Friend-Johnston

Library and Archives Canada Cataloguing in Publication

Casineanu, Gabriela, 1961—, author

Metaphors: An Emotional Journey, 1st ed.

ISBN: 978-1-9994249-7-8 (paperback)

ISBN: 978-1-9994249-8-5 (hardcover)

ISBN: 978-1-9994249-9-2 (ebook)

PRAISE FOR THIS BOOK

A beautiful journey of transformation.

~ Paola

So much insight and meaning.

~ Gervend

Such feelings of hope and light!

~ Jolie

Thank you for your universal and timely journey!

~ Robyn

Powerful, insightful, and full of life. Thank you.

~ Haleh

Touching! We all could find ourselves in this visual journey.

~ Bianca

A suggestive expression of the sensibility of a good and sincere soul!

~ Remus

Beautiful work Gabriela. Thank you for your light, positivity and generosity.

~ Sam

*To anyone who deals with a job loss,
divorce or other major setback in their life.*

CONTENTS

1. My Heart Fell into Pieces — 1
2. Wind of Change — 3
3. Uncertainty — 5
4. Escape — 7
5. The Unknown — 9
6. Longing for Light — 11
7. Going With the Flow — 13
8. Lightening the Darker Corners of My Soul — 15
9. Past Shadows — 17
10. Burst of Joy — 19
11. New Path — 21
12. Stand Out — 23
13. Enjoy — 25
14. Rebirth — 27
15. Perseverance — 29
16. Crack the Twilight Zone — 31

Afterword — 33
About the Author — 39
Also by Gabriela Casineanu — 41

EPIGRAPH

You're about to embark on a journey: a visual representation of an emotional journey I went through at the beginning of 2012.

While short, it was very intense and... inspiring! At least that's what I noticed a year later when I looked back.

While going through the nature photographs I took for a solo exhibition, some images stood out! It was as though they wanted to grab my attention... to teach me nature metaphors of human nature!

They "told" me what I've been through. Like puzzle pieces of emotions at first, which rearranged themselves in a sequence that portrayed my emotional journey after suddenly losing a job.

Now I'm curious: will these images bring up emotions or *speak* to you as well?

~ Gabriela

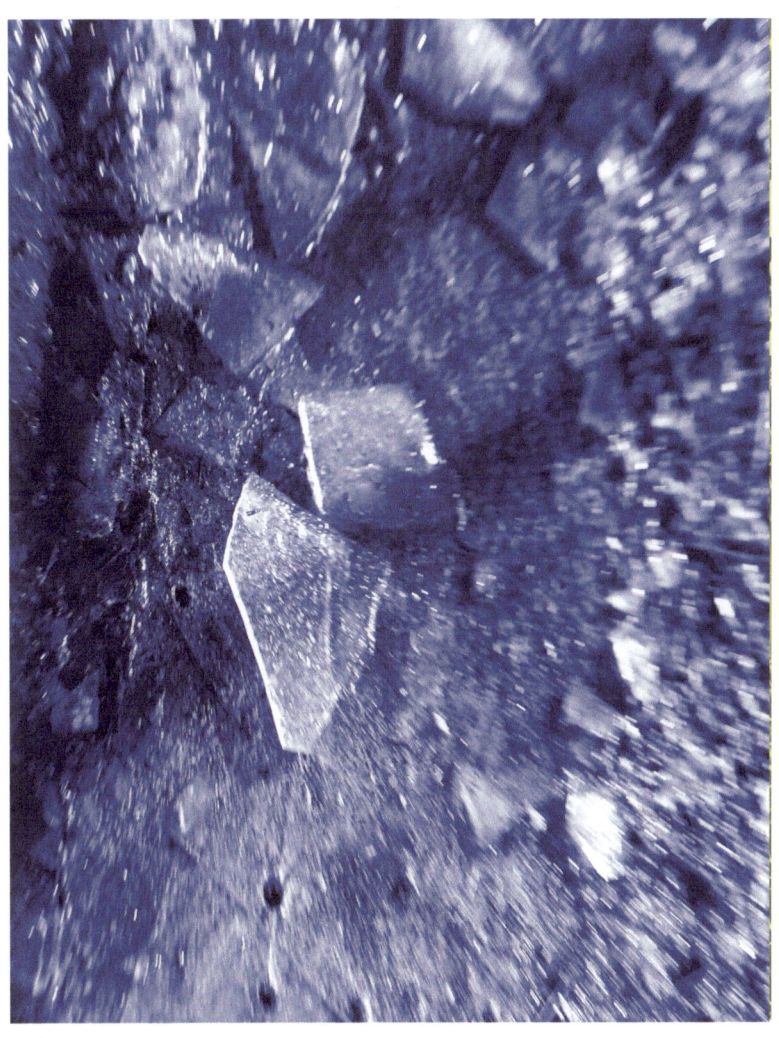

The day I was told I didn't have a job anymore
my heart fell into pieces ...

Obviously, a wind of change was blowing ...

... but the uncertainty was overwhelming.

To be honest,
I had wanted to escape for a long time ...

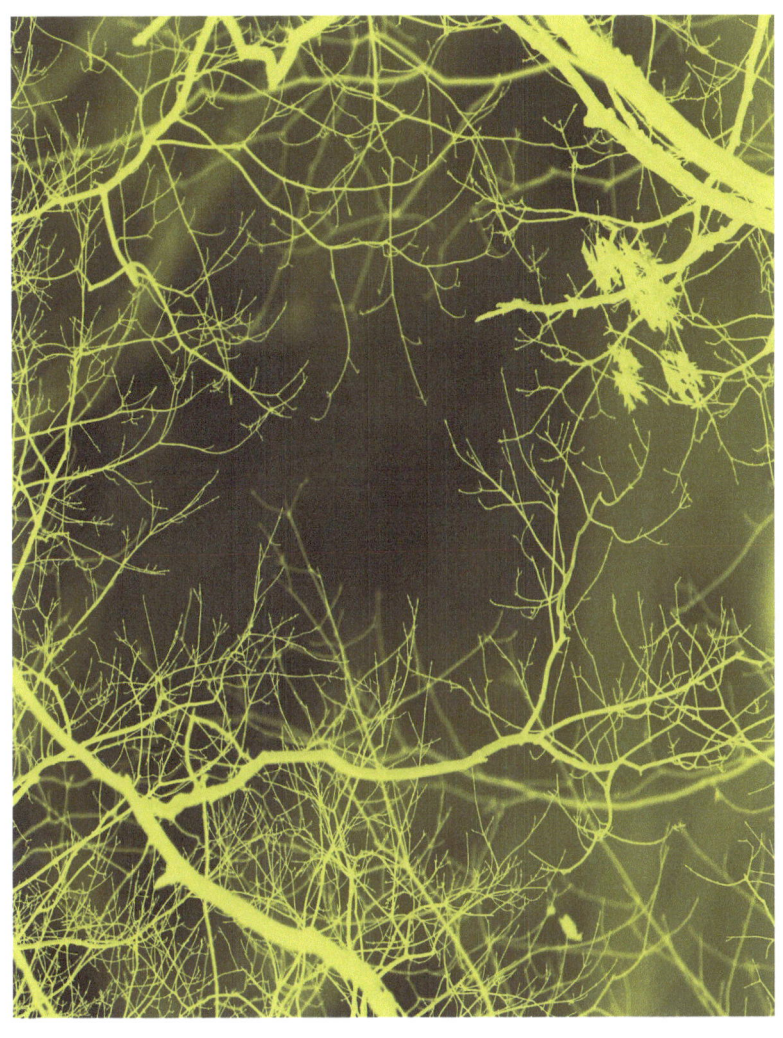

... but going into the unknown was scary.

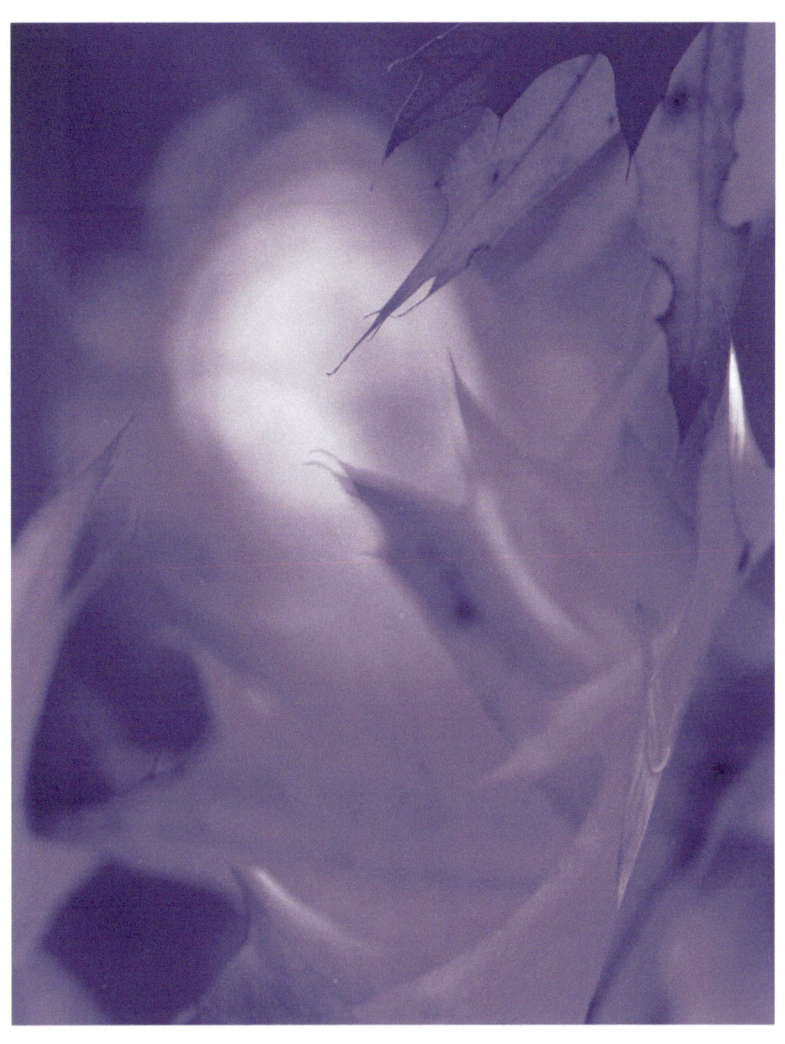

I was longing for light …

... now struggling to go with the flow.

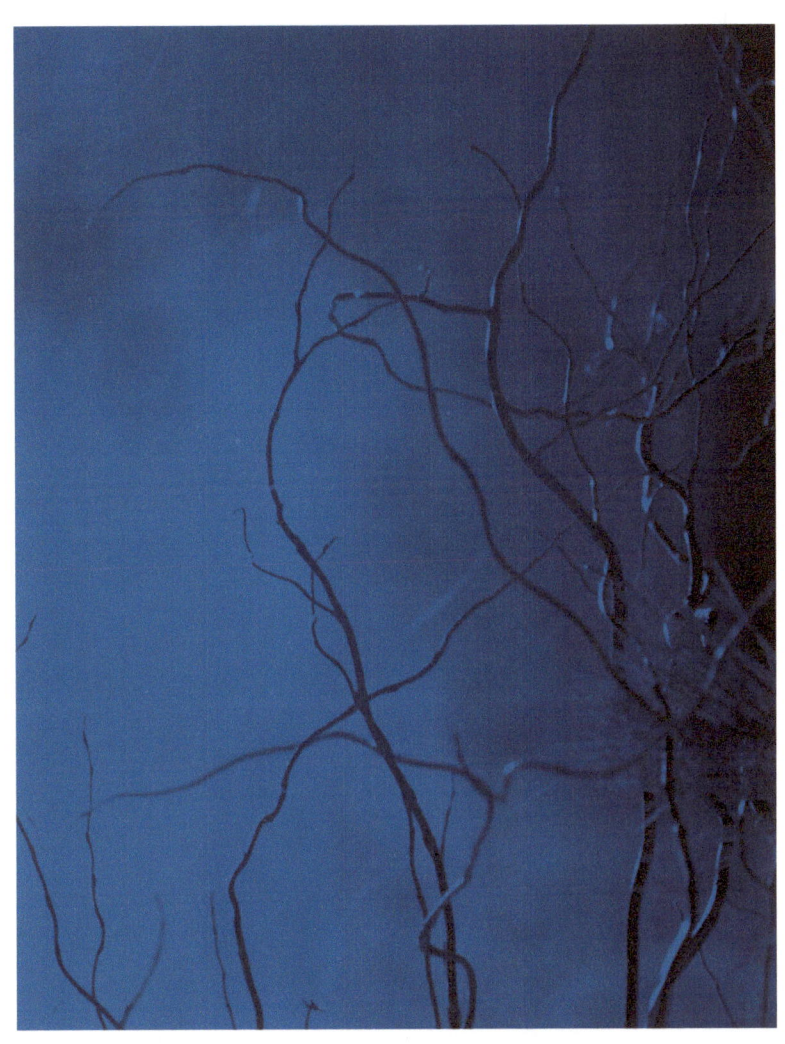

Throwing some light
into the darker corners of my soul ...

... and overcoming past shadows ...

... a burst of joy came suddenly to the surface.

It was time to embrace the new path opening for me wherever it would take me.

I put to work my strengths, will, and talents
to stand out ...

... and enjoy ...

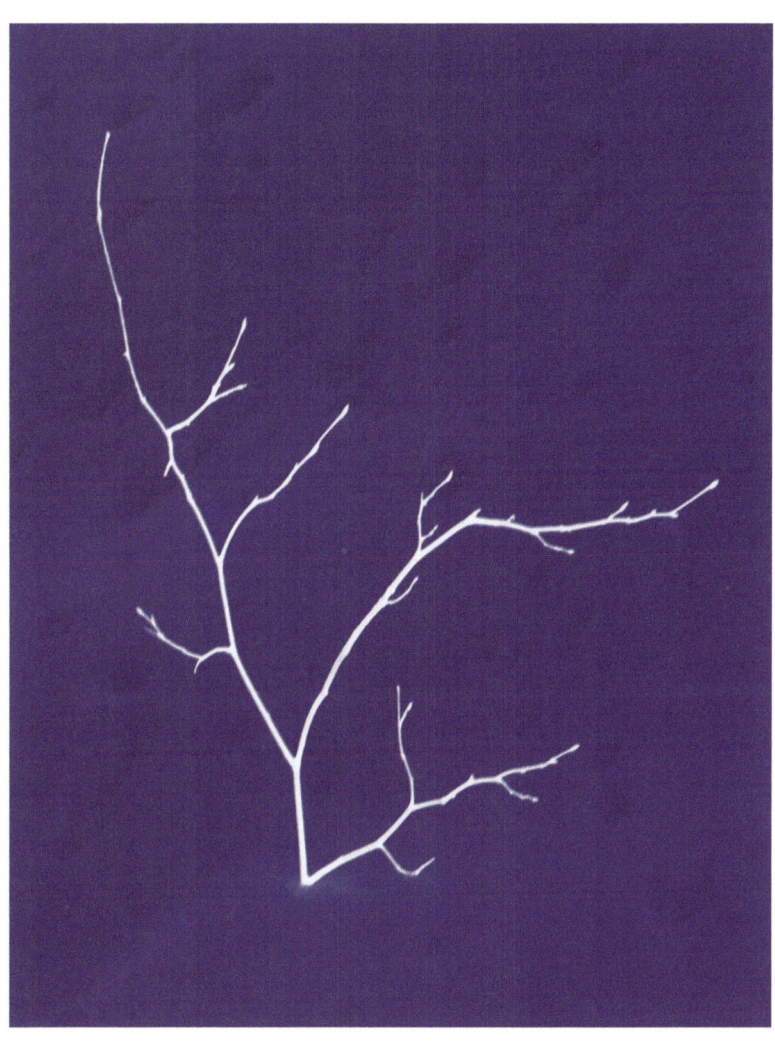

... my rebirth.

And with perseverance ...

... to crack the twilight zone toward a better future!

AFTERWORD

We go through life experiencing a range of emotions. They're like the waves of the ocean: coming... receding... but only if we're skilled enough to let them go. Otherwise, we trap them inside in a darker corner of our soul. They're not meant to be there, they're not part of us!

Some come to the surface when we least expect, triggered by similar conditions that brought them in the first place. Are we ready to let them go? Are we able to let them go skillfully, without harming those around us?

Some prefer to stuff them inside, continuing to carry them within... until they raise their *head* again, begging to be let go. And they stuff them inside again, unconsciously causing inner suffering—which could lead to physical and mental illness.

Some emotions are pleasant, others are not. Some sneak inside us without noticing; we can pick up emotions from those around us, or even from those who inhabited the same space for a while.

In childhood, are we taught how to deal with our emotions? As far as I remember, the school system didn't. Family and friends did their best with what they knew. Most of us heard that some emotions are bad, they aren't acceptable—neither inside nor expressed. So we repress them, adding more and more to the emotional burden we accumulate over the years.

However, experiencing emotions is part of what makes us humans. If we become aware of their transitory nature—and learn how to let them go—we can surf their waves throughout life, making it a more healthy and enjoyable journey.

"How long did it take you to go through all these emotions?" asked me someone who saw the *Metaphors* exhibit.

"Two days. But I don't wish anyone to experience this deep and agonizing emotional journey" I replied, remembering how it all started.

I'm someone who rarely cries. That day, in the manager's office, I handled quite well the news that they eliminated my position (because of government funding cuts) until…

"I really appreciated your work, you did a great job… " said my supervisor, who just came back from a month vacation, allowing me to coordinate the team in her absence.

An unknown rage grew from inside, almost ready to explode: "Then why do you let me go, while keeping the person you hired only six months ago? I've been with the organization for almost five years!" Without saying a word, my rage found its way out through tears. As much I wanted to hold them back, I couldn't.

"Since you're a permanent employee…" said the manager, "… we're giving you two options: you either leave or take over the position of the colleague who has similar tasks in another team. We need your answer in two days!"

"How come you're asking me to choose? Aren't the managers supposed to make such decisions?" Again, I swallowed my words in anger.

In a moment, I realized why he didn't want to make that decision himself: forcing me to accept the other position meant he was not responsible for throwing my colleague on the streets. He knew that she wouldn't be able to get another job because of her temporary work visa, received only for that position. She was also in the middle of a difficult divorce, with three small children relying on her since the husband was not willing to pay for child support.

With growing anger toward how they handled the situation, I became an emotional wreck. Before stepping into his office, I was still excited about the previous week spent at my son's house, where I gave the first bath to their cute baby.

Tears rolling on my face, I left the manager's office. Two days of agony followed, trying to figure out what's best to do.

My situation was not rosy either. Charging my credit cards for the training and expensive workshops I took for my career change (from engineering to coaching) left a big hole in my bank account and no savings. Should I also mention the monthly mortgage and car payments I still had to pay?

Nonetheless, taking over my colleague's position—while her situation was more difficult—was even less appealing. Plus, she was the only colleague with whom I got along very well; we often talked about her situation, encouraging her when it was hard to bear—knowing firsthand how hard and painful it is to go through a divorce with small children.

During those two days, I desperately asked the Universe for a sign to help me make the right decision. And it came—in the form of a dream—the day I was supposed to let them know my decision. I had such a painful, vivid dream that morning (it's still ingrained in my memory): I was lying on a surface in a darkish foggy room when two fierce creatures came close. Fighting for me, each grabbed me by one leg... beginning to tear me apart! The pain became so unbearable that I woke up, with tears still falling down my cheeks. At that moment, a subtle thought came to mind, bringing with it so much peace and joy! I knew for sure what was best decision. That thought gave me the courage to step into the unknown, walking the new path that opened ahead. I felt free!

Suddenly, focusing on building my business was so exciting! Although I had no clue how I would survive since I didn't even have money to invite potential clients for a coffee.

However, I survived—even though the first two years were hard. I ended up paying all my debt while building my coaching business and getting some jobs here and there.

The bonus of this journey?

It opened my artistic path, and even helped it... financially!

The organization that showed me the door in 2012 invited me to have a solo photo exhibition at their art gallery. This exhibit —made possible with the financial support of the Ontario Arts Council—made me become an *emerging artist* accepted in the mentoring program of The Art Laboratory (Le Labo).

Some of the nature photographs I took during that mentoring project were *speaking* to me. Jotting down their insights, they became the puzzle pieces that rearranged themselves into a *visual expression of my emotional journey*. Since I love colours, I was not too happy with the original photos (taken between November 2012 and March 2013), which had only grey nuances. However, playing with photo-editing software, I stumbled upon the option to change image colours—which made them better suited to project a certain mood or feeling.

This *emotional journey* became the *Metaphors* exhibition—presented with the financial support from Le Labo and Ontario Arts Council, part of the CONTACT Photography Festival Toronto in 2013.

It's the same *emotional journey* presented in this book. I created it also as an invitation to look at nature as a source of inspiration, energy and resilience—as I experienced many times in the past. As an introvert, nature is my best friend! It always helps me when I'm down, either physically or mentally! It even gives me ideas, sometimes. It helped me navigate more easily the first years after I immigrated to Canada—when hiking and nature photography were my refuge.

I love to turn simple symbols found in nature into metaphors of the human spirit! My passion for combining visuals with text—to make abstract concepts more tangible—lead to creating the Photo-coaching book series. I strongly believe that —beyond the visual aspect—photography is a great medium for expressing meaningful and intentional connections that might be easily missed in such a stressful world.

Speaking of the world, I'm curious:

Did any of the images in this book catch your attention in particular?

I'm sure—if I had kept that anger and rage—I wouldn't have been so open and able to perceive that subtle thought, which made me realize what was the best decision for me.

When I put together those photographs, what resonated with me the most was the white tree that stood out in the forest—showing its strength—differentiating itself from the rest of the trees. That's what I also needed in that moment: to rely on my strengths to overcome that challenge!

A visitor to the Metaphors exhibition resonated with the

image portraying the purple path going into the forest. Because of the struggles she encountered while pursuing her passion, she was about to quit that path. That photograph changed her mind, making her curious where the path will lead her if she sticks with it longer.

The images in this book that resonated with you reflect emotions you're still holding on, consciously or unconsciously.

What do you need to let them go?

There's a beautiful path waiting for you when you let go, as my poem and experience show:

The Journey
~ by Gabriela Casineanu

The day I was told I didn't have a job anymore my heart fell into pieces.
Obviously, a wind of change was blowing…
… but the uncertainty was overwhelming.
To be honest, I had wanted to escape for a long time…
… but going into the unknown was scary.
I was longing for light…
… now struggling with going with the flow.
Throwing some light into the darker corners of my soul…
… and overcoming past shadows…
… a burst of joy came suddenly to the surface.
It was time to embrace the new path opening for me, wherever it would take me.
I put to work my strengths, will and talents to stand out…
… and enjoy…
… my rebirth.
And with perseverance …
… to crack the twilight zone toward a better future!

ABOUT THE AUTHOR

Gabriela Casineanu has successfully overcome several life challenges and career transitions. She started her professional path in electronic engineering, then added entrepreneurship, coaching, artistic expressions, and writing... continuing to explore life with the curiosity of a child!

With a daily meditation practice, and a passion for personal growth and nature photography, Gabriela relies on intuition to guide her next steps. She writes books she would have liked to read to help her navigate life more easily.

More about Gabriela, her books, and updates:
GabrielaCasineanu.com

Video (1:41 min.): *Metaphors* exhibit opening event (2013)
youtu.be/sedBtUoUWtY

ALSO BY GABRIELA CASINEANU

Please leave an honest review for
Metaphors: An Emotional Journey
to help others understand
what the book is about.

OTHER BOOKS

https://gabrielacasineanu.com/book

Introvert Strengths Series

Job Search Series

 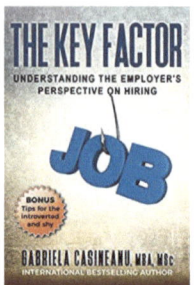 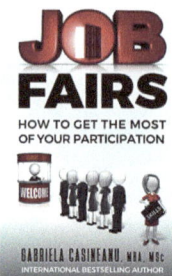

Photo-Coaching (Self-Coaching) Series

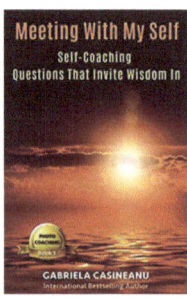  

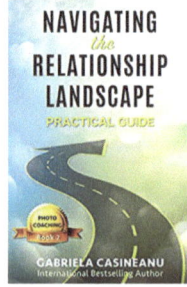  

To receive notifications about Gabriela's **upcoming books**:

GabrielaCasineanu.com/series

COACHING, CONSULTING, SPEAKING

GabrielaCasineanu.com

www.ingramcontent.com/pod-product-compliance
Lightning Source LLC
Chambersburg PA
CBHW041217070526
44583CB00001B/12